飞向中文
Flying with Chinese

4A Student Book

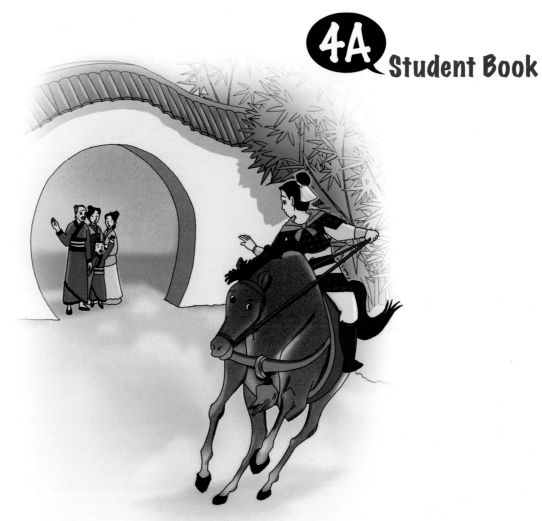

Shuhan C. Wang, Ph. D. • Carol Ann Dahlberg, Ph. D.
Chiachyi Chiu, M.A. • Marisa Fang, M.S. • Mei-Ju Hwang, Ed.D.

Marshall Cavendish
Education

Published by Marshall Cavendish Education
An imprint of Marshall Cavendish

The Publisher
Panpac Education Private Limited
(a member of Marshall Cavendish Publishing Group)
Times Centre, 1 New Industrial Road,
Singapore 536196.
Tel: (65) 6411 0820
Fax: (65) 6846 3440
Email: panpmktg@panpaceducation.com
Website: http://www.panpaceducation.com

Distributed in North America by:

CHENG & TSUI COMPANY
Bringing Asia to the World™

Cheng & Tsui Company,
25 West St, Boston, MA 02111
www.cheng-tsui.com
Toll Free 1-800-554-1963

Other Marshall Cavendish Offices:
Marshall Cavendish Ltd. 119 Wardour Street, London W1F 0UW, UK • Marshall Cavendish Corporation. 99 White Plains Road, Tarrytown NY 10591-9001, USA • Marshall Cavendish International (Thailand) Co Ltd. 253 Asoke, 12th Flr, Sukhumvit 21 Road, Klongtoey Nua, Wattana, Bangkok 10110, Thailand • Marshall Cavendish (Malaysia) Sdn Bhd, Times Subang, Lot 46, Subang Hi-Tech Industrial Park, Batu Tiga, 40000 Shah Alam, Selangor Darul Ehsan, Malaysia • Marshall Cavendish Book Culture (Beijing) Co Ltd. 10B, 10th Floor Guoying Gongyu Building No. 38 Hou Guang Ping, Hutong Xicheng District, Beijing China 100035 • Times Publishing (Hong Kong) Limited. Unit 02, 30/F Citicorp Centre 18 Whitfield Road Causeway Bay Hong Kong • MC East Ltd. 9/11 Korpus 2 Dmitria Ulanova Moscow 117036 Russian Federation

Marshall Cavendish is a trademark of Times Publishing Limited

ISBN 978-981-01-6727-1

First published 2008

Publisher: Lim Geok Leng
Editors: Yvonne Lee   Richard Soh   Chong Liping   Cao Zichen
Chief Designer: Roy Foo

Printed by Times Graphics Pte Ltd

Preface

Flying with Chinese is a series designed to make the most of children's natural ability to learn language by creating meaningful contexts for learning and guiding them towards language proficiency, literacy development and cultural appreciation. Each book is based on a theme and integrated with other subject areas in the elementary school curriculum.

Flying with Chinese is standards-based and focuses on learners' performance. Some of the important elements in this series include the following:
1. Thematic planning and instruction, with emphasis on the principles and structure of a good story;
2. "Standards for Chinese Language Learning", which is part of the _Standards for Foreign Language Learning in the 21st Century_ ;
3. Principles of _Understanding by Design_ ;
4. Matching languages with children (_Languages and Children: Making the Match_).

Under three umbrella themes, each book in the series takes on a different but related sub-theme. These themes are interesting to the learners, connect with the curriculum of the elementary school, promote understanding of Chinese culture, and provide a context for language use.

The Student Book provides the basic story for the lessons, while the Workbook gives learners the opportunity to practice the language and use the concepts presented in the Student Book. The Teacher Guide suggests activities for each day and indicates when the Workbook pages are to be used.

Flying with Chinese focuses on a group of children who are learning Chinese together. These children and their families come from a wide range of backgrounds, and several are heritage Chinese speakers. One member of the group goes to China with her family, where she attends a Chinese school and shares her experiences with her former classmates. Throughout the series, learners are introduced to legends, real and fictional characters of importance to Chinese culture, and significant customs, celebrations, and other elements of the Chinese way of life.

Flying with Chinese can be used independently or as part of a sequence of study in a program. Just as a child can fly a kite on his own or in a group, we hope that children will have fun flying these Chinese kites while gaining insight into the Chinese-speaking world.

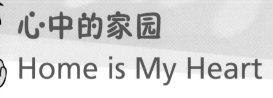

心中的家园
Home is My Heart

目录 Contents

预备课 大家一起来拼音

放调号规则一

你知道吗？如果你用拼音，声调要加在韵母上，例如：a, o, e, i, u, ü。

放调号规则二

如果有两个或者三个母音，放调号的规则是这样的：

调号放在第一个韵母上面。	ài	áo	ān	ǎng
	ēi	ěn	èng	
	ōng	óu		
可是如果开头有 i，u，ü，调号要放在它们后面的韵母上。	iá	iǎo	iè	iū
	iǒng	ián	iǎng	
	uà	uāi	uǎn	
	uáng	uǐ	uén	
	uǒ	uán	üè	

拼音规则

如果 i 是第一个声音，y 就要加在 i 前面。	i → yi in → yin ing → ying
如果 ü 是第一个声音，y 也要加在 ü 前面。	ü → yu üe → yue ün → yun
如果 u 是第一个声音，w 就要加在 u 前面。	ua → wa uo → wo uai → wai
如果 uei 前面有声母，uei 就要变成 ui。	duei → dui huei → hui

如果 uen 前面有声母，uen 就要变成 un。	kuen → kun guen → gun shuen → shun
如果 ü 的前面是 j，q，x，ü 就要变成 u。	jü → ju qü → qu xü → xu
如果 ü 的前面是 n，l，ü 还是 ü。	nü → nü lü → lü
如果 iou 的前面有声母，iou 就变成 iu。	niou → niu jiou → jiu qiou → qiu

变音规则

当你看到调号时，基本上就要照着念。可是，有时候要变调。

三声的变调	
三声—三声 → 二声—三声	nǐ hǎo → níhǎo xiǎo gǒu → xiáogǒu

"一"的 变调	
自己是一声	yī (一)
在四声前念二声	yí dìng (一定) yí kuài qián (一块钱)
其它都是第四声	yì tiān (一天) yì nián (一年)

"不" 的变调

自己是四声	bù (不)
在四声前念二声	bú duì (不对) bú qù (不去)
其它都是第四声	bù hǎo (不好) bù xǐ huan (不喜欢)

轻声

有时候有些音节念得很轻，不带调，叫轻声，常常是第二个音节。	bà ba (爸爸) mā ma (妈妈) tā de (他的) lái le (来了)

我知道还有一个，就是花木兰啊！

是的，花木兰也是中国很有名的女性。你们知道花木兰有什么贡献吗？

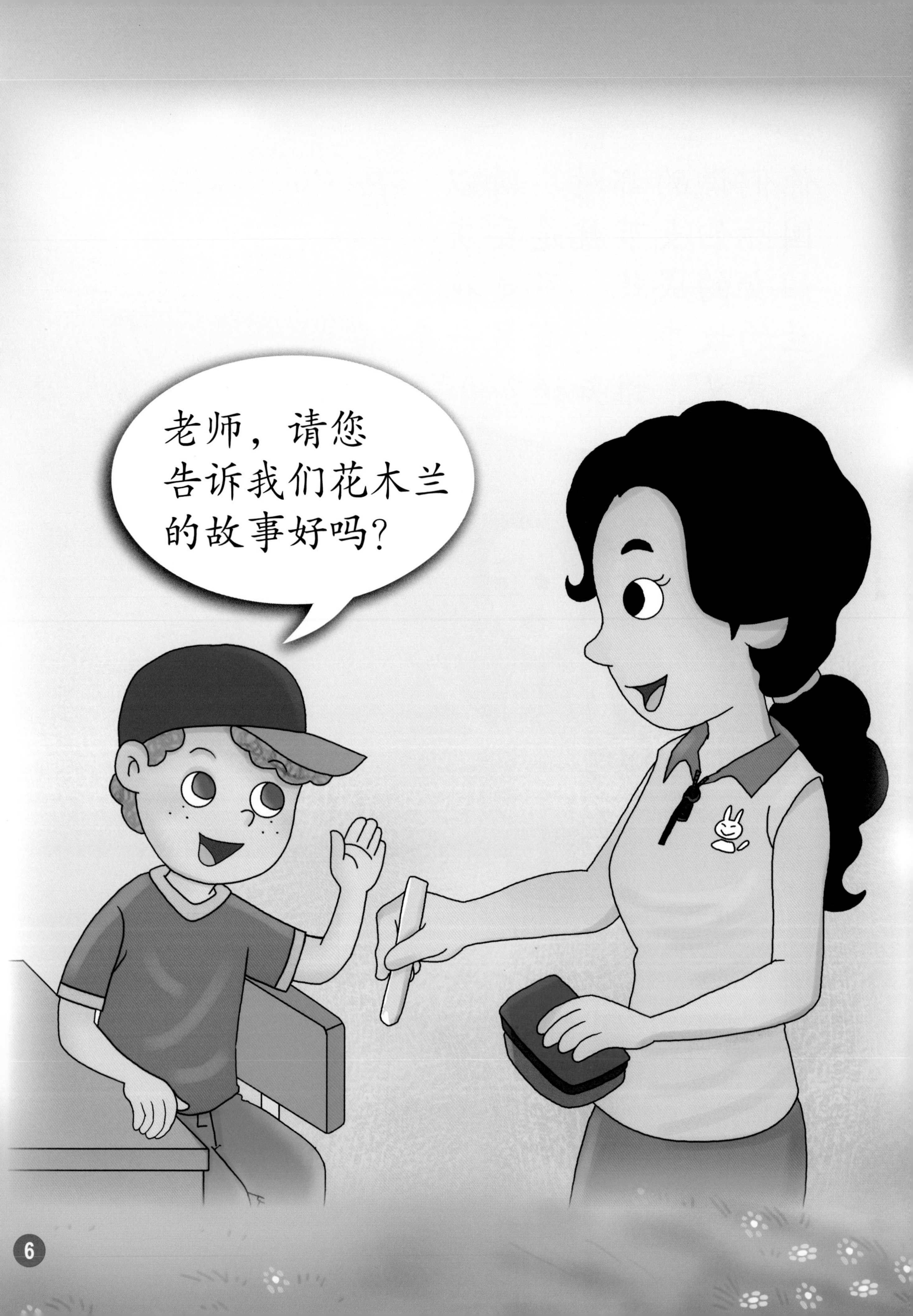
老师，请您
告诉我们花木兰
的故事好吗？

 我会认

兰
lán

家
jiā

庭
tíng

 拼音和声调练习

花 木 兰
huā mù lán

妇 女 节
fù nǚ jié

贡 献
gòng xiàn

意 义
yì yì

家 庭
jiā tíng

成 就
chéng jiù

拼音挑战

庆祝	国际	女性
另一个	告诉	打仗

I can do these things in Chinese, can you?

I can...

❖ tell someone about a few famous Chinese women

❖ call people's attention and start a topic, using "你知道……吗? "

❖ explain what is International Women's Day

❖ tell what I can do, using "可以"

❖ write 兰、家、庭 and other *hanzi* learned previously and use them to write labels, signs and notes. I can do this either by handwriting or using keyboard.

敌人来了

古时候，在一个小村庄里，有一个家庭。
这家的主人姓花，以前是个大将军。

花将军有两个女儿和一个小儿子。

二女儿木兰长得又漂亮又聪明。她不但会织布绣花，而且还会骑马射箭。

有一天，木兰正在练习剑术。她有个地方不太明白，就急忙去问她父亲。

爹，刚才我在练习剑术，有个地方不太明白，您可以再教我吗？

可是外面有草原，有树林，有河流，可以骑马和打猎，也可以练习新剑术。

就在这个时候，外面传来了一阵敲门声
"砰砰砰！砰砰砰！"。木兰把门打开，
两个将士走了进来。

练
liàn

纟 纟 纟 纩 纩
练 练 练

习
xí

フ 刁 习

帮
bāng

一 二 三 丰 邦
邦 邦 帮 帮

拼音和声调练习

骑 马　　　 打 猎　　　 女 儿
qí mǎ　　　 dǎ liè　　　 nǔ ér

漂 亮　　　 将 军　　　 聪 明
piào liang　　 jiāng jūn　　 cōng míng

主人	织布	将军
练习	剑术	帮忙

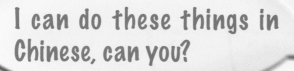

I can do these things in Chinese, can you?

I can...

❖ tell the different responsibilities of a male and a female in ancient China

❖ describe two qualities of someone or something, using "又......又......"

❖ emphasize two qualities of someone or something, using "不但......而且"

❖ write 练、习、帮 and other *hanzi* learned previously and use them to write labels, signs and notes. I can do this either by handwriting or using keyboard.

代父从军

花将军非常烦恼，因为他年纪大了，可是儿子又太小，不能替他去打仗。

21

第二天，木兰向家人告别。虽然战场很危险，但是她很勇敢。她希望能很快地打胜仗，早早回家和家人团聚。

代 dài
ノ　イ　イ　代　代

从 cóng
ノ　ナ　从　从

军 jūn
丶　宀　冖　军　军　军

拼音和声调练习

烦	恼		年	纪		认	得
fán	nǎo		nián	jì		rèn	dé
请	问		危	险		辛	苦
qǐng	wèn		wēi	xiǎn		xīn	kǔ

26

不行	办法	问题
代替	勇敢	团聚

I can do these things in Chinese, can you?

I can...

❖ tell someone that something is dangerous and tell someone not to worry about me

❖ introduce a question, using "请问"

❖ make an explanation, using "因为……"

❖ make a comment by providing another point of view, using "虽然……但是……"

❖ write 代、从、军 and other *hanzi* learned previously and use them to write labels, signs and notes. I can do this either by handwriting or using keyboard.

如果你是木兰……

木兰的军队有时在长城防守，有时在山洞里埋伏，有时在树林里打仗。

由于木兰的勇敢和聪明，他们的军队打了很多胜仗。过了几年，他们终于打败了敌人。木兰也被升为大将军。

皇帝很高兴，要赏木兰许多金银财宝，并且要让她做大官。

可是，木兰不要金银财宝，也不要求做大官。她只向皇帝要求了一样东西。

我会要求皇帝送我一匹马，我可以在大草原上奔跑。

因为木兰很想念她的家人，还有家乡的草原和树林，她可以在那儿骑马打猎。

因为木兰很孝顺，她想回家照顾年老的父母。

老师，如果您是木兰，您会想要什么呢？

如果我是木兰，我也想要求回家，因为家是世界上最温暖、最甜蜜的地方。这就是木兰故事的另一个意义。

其实，我们每一个人心中都有一个
"故乡"，就是自己生长的家园。
你们回家问问你们的父母或爷爷
奶奶，他们的故乡在哪儿？

故
gù

乡
xiāng

求
qiú

拼音和声调练习

皇	帝	骆	驼	家	乡
huáng	dì	luò	tuó	jiā	xiāng
沙	漠	旅	行	金	银
shā	mò	lǚ	xíng	jīn	yín

如果	长城	长江
黄河	要求	孝顺

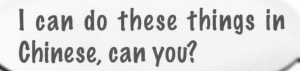

I can do these things in Chinese, can you?

I can...

❖ talk about what would one do in a conditional situation, using "如果......会"

❖ identify different modes of transportations for different purposes

❖ give examples to explain the Chinese concept of "孝顺"

❖ retell Hua Mulan's story, via acting or using props or pictures

❖ write 故、乡、求 and other *hanzi* learned previously and use them to write labels, signs and notes. I can do this either by handwriting or using keyboard.

遥远的故乡

我的家乡在太平洋边。以前，我常常和同学到海边拣贝壳，看日落。我也很想念我的故乡。

老师，您的故乡在哪儿呢？

我会认

想 xiǎng
一 十 才 木 机 机 机
相 相 相 想 想 想

时 shí
丨 冂 月 日 旦 时 时

候 hòu
丿 亻 亻 伫 伫 伫 候
伫 候 候

拼音和声调练习

雨	林		美	国		墨	西	哥
yǔ	lín		měi	guó		mò	xī	gē

日	本		非	洲		太	平	洋
rì	běn		fēi	zhōu		tài	píng yáng

西湖	想要	回家
鳄鱼	热带	日本

I can do these things in Chinese, can you?

I can...

❖ talk about my hometown and an experience I had when I was little

❖ identify several countries in the world

❖ name 长城, 长江, 黄河 and 西湖 on a map of China

❖ write 想、时、候 and other *hanzi* learned previously and use them to write labels, signs and notes. I can do this either by handwriting or using keyboard.

老师，您为什么要来美国呢？

我是来美国念书的。因为我喜欢美国的环境，所以留在这里。你们看，很多人从世界各地来美国，在美国建立自己的新家，这就是"四海一家"的意义。

我的家庭

我的 家庭真　可爱 春夏秋冬都舒畅大家

一起多　快乐 大家 一起多欢 笑

可　爱　的　家　庭啊　　你给

我　爱和 希望我会 永远爱着　你

我会认

留
liú

认
rèn

识
shí

拼音和声调练习

自　由　　进　步　　决　定
zì　yóu　　jìn　bù　　jué　dìng

结　婚　　工　作　　环　境
jié　hūn　　gōng　zuò　　huán　jìng

拼音挑战

| 工程师 | 医生 | 护士 |
| 念书 | 知识 | 四海一家 |

I can do these things in Chinese, can you?

I can...

- ❖ ask people why they came to America

- ❖ give two reasons why immigrants choose to stay in America, using "因为......所以......"

- ❖ talk about a female figure whom I admire and give reasons

- ❖ talk about two big ideas I learned from Hua Mulan's story

- ❖ explain the Chinese proverb "四海一家"

- ❖ sing the song "我的家庭" with the class

- ❖ write 留、认、识 and other *hanzi* learned previously and use them to write labels, signs and notes. I can do this either by handwriting or using keyboard.

大家一起来！

兰
lán

家
jiā

庭
tíng

练
liàn

习
xí

帮
bāng

代
dài

从
cóng

军
jūn

故 gù

乡 xiāng

求 qiú

想 xiǎng

时 shí

候 hòu

留 liú

认 rèn

识 shí

词汇表
Vocabulary List

Hanzi	Pinyin	English	Page
Lesson 1			
知道	zhī dào	to know	1
今天	jīn tiān	today	1
日子	rì zi	day	1
国际	guó jì	international	1
妇女节	fù nǚ jié	Women's Day	1
有名的	yǒu míng de	famous	2
女性	nǚ xìng	female	2
养蚕	yǎng cán	to raise silkworms	2
取丝	qǔ sī	to collect silk	2
贡献	gòng xiàn	to contribute	3
打仗	dǎ zhàng	to fight a war	4

Hanzi	Pinyin	English	Page
家庭	jiā tíng	family	4
国家	guó jiā	country	4
做家事	zuò jiā shì	to do house chores	4
做大事	zuò dà shì	to do something important	4
都	dōu	all	5
庆祝	qìng zhù	to celebrate	5
成就	chéng jiù	accomplishment	5
故事	gù shi	story	5
另一个	lìng yí gè	another	5
意义	yì yì	significance; meaning	5
Lesson 2			
古时候	gǔ shí hou	in olden times; in ancient times	9
村庄	cūn zhuāng	village	9
主人	zhǔ rén	master of a household; patriarch	9

Hanzi	Pinyin	English	Page
以前是	yǐ qián shì	used to be	9
将军	jiāng jūn	(military) general	9
女儿	nǔ ér	daughter	10
儿子	ér zi	son	10
织布	zhī bù	to weave	11
绣花	xiù huā	to embroider	11
骑马	qí mǎ	to ride a horse	11
射箭	shè jiàn	to do archery	11
练习	liàn xí	to practice	12
剑术	jiàn shù	(martial arts) sword movements	12
明白	míng bai	clear; understand	12
急忙	jí máng	in a hurry, hurriedly	12
父亲	fù qīn	father	12
爹	diē	father (traditional form)	12

Hanzi	Pinyin	English	Page
刚才	gāng cái	just now	12
应该	yīng gāi	must; ought to	13
帮忙	bāng máng	to help	13
往外跑	wǎng wài pǎo	to go out	13
草原	cǎo yuán	grassland; prairie	14
树林	shù lín	woods	14
河流	hé liú	river	14
打猎	dǎ liè	hunting	14
敲门	qiāo mén	to knock on the door	15
把门打开	bǎ mén dǎ kāi	to open the door	15
将士	jiàng shì	officer	15
敌人	dí rén	enemy	16
攻打	gōng dǎ	to attack	16
皇帝	huáng dì	emperor	16

Hanzi	Pinyin	English	Page
立刻	lì kè	right away; immediately	16
报到	bào dào	to report for duty	16
Lesson 3			
代父从军	dài fù cóng jūn	(an idiom) Hua Mulan joined the army for her father	19
非常	fēi cháng	extremely	19
烦恼	fán nǎo	worried	19
因为	yīn wèi	because	19
年纪	nián jì	age	19
可是	kě shì	but	19
替	tì	to replace	19
请问	qǐng wèn	(asking a question) excuse me	20
你找谁？	nǐ zhǎo shéi	Whom are you looking for?	20

Hanzi	Pinyin	English	Page
在家	zài jiā	at home	20
有什么事吗？	yǒu shén me shì ma	May I help you?	21
娘	niáng	mother (traditional form)	21
认得	rèn dé	to recognize	21
打扮	dǎ bàn	to dress up	22
男生	nán shēng	boy	22
代替	dài tì	to replace	22
不行	bù xíng	not workable	23
女孩子	nǚ hái zi	girl	23
怎么	zěn me	how	23
又…又	yòu…yòu	as…as; both…and	23
危险	wēi xiǎn	dangerous	23
辛苦	xīn kǔ	difficult; laborious	23

tHanzi	Pinyin	English	Page
让	ràng	let	23
只有	zhǐ yǒu	only (someone or something) can...	24
才是	cái shì	only (someone or something) is...	24
认不出来	rèn bù chu lai	cannot recognize	24
不会	bú huì	will not	24
问题	wèn tí	problem	24
向…告别	xiàng...gào bié	to say good-bye to (someone)	25
虽然…但是	suī rán...dàn shì	although..., ...	25
战场	zhàn chǎng	battlefield	25
勇敢	yǒng gǎn	brave	25
希望	xī wàng	to wish; to hope	25
很快地	hěn kuài de	soon	25

Hanzi	Pinyin	English	Page
打胜仗	dǎ shèng zhàng	to win the battle	25
团聚	tuán jù	to reunite	25
Lesson 4			
如果	rú guǒ	if	28
军队	jūn duì	army; troop	28
有时	yǒu shí	sometimes	28
长城	cháng chéng	the Great Wall of China	28
防守	fáng shǒu	to defend; to guard	28
山洞	shān dòng	cave	28
埋伏	mái fú	to ambush; to trap	28
聪明	cōng míng	intelligent	29
过了几年	guò le jǐ nián	after several years	29
终于	zhōng yú	finally	29
打败了	dǎ bài le	defeated	29

Hanzi	Pinyin	English	Page
被升为…	bèi shēng wéi	was promoted to be	29
赏	shǎng	to reward	30
金银财宝	jīn yín cái bǎo	treasures	30
并且	bìng qiě	in addition	30
做大官	zuò dà guān	to be a high-ranking officer	30
向…要求	xiàng…yāo qiú	ask (someone) for (something)	31
一样东西	yí yàng dōng xi	one thing	31
送	sòng	to give	33
一匹马	yì pǐ mǎ	a horse	33
奔跑	bēn pǎo	to gallop	33
一条船	yì tiáo chuán	a ship	34
长江	cháng jiāng	Yangtze River	34
黄河	huáng hé	Yellow River	34

Hanzi	Pinyin	English	Page
一只骆驼	yì zhī luò tuó	a camel	35
沙漠	shā mò	desert	35
旅行	lǚ xíng	to travel	35
只要	zhǐ yào	only wanted	36
想念	xiǎng niàn	to miss	37
孝顺	xiào shùn	to obey parents; to show filial piety to parents	37
照顾	zhào gù	to look after or take care of	37
年老的	nián lǎo de	elderly	37
父母	fù mǔ	parents	37
世界上	shì jiè shang	in the world	38
最	zuì	~ est, most	38
温暖	wēn nuǎn	warm	38
甜蜜	tián mì	sweet	38

Hanzi	Pinyin	English	Page
地方	dì fang	place	38
其实	qí shí	in fact	39
心中	xīn zhōng	in the hearts of	39
故乡	gù xiāng	hometown	39
自己	zì jǐ	self	39
生长	shēng zhǎng	to grow	39
家园	jiā yuán	homeland	39
爷爷	yé ye	grandfather	39
奶奶	nǎi nai	grandmother	39
Lesson 5			
遥远	yáo yuǎn	distant; far away	42
墨西哥	mò xī gē	Mexico	42
长大	zhǎng dà	to grow up	42
那里	nà lǐ	there	42

Hanzi	Pinyin	English	Page
有	yǒu	there is; there are	42
大片的	dà piàn de	massive	42
热带	rè dài	tropical	42
雨林	yǔ lín	rainforest	42
小时候	xiǎo shí hou	when … was young	43
常常	cháng cháng	frequently	43
还会	hái huì	also will	43
碰到	pèng dào	to come across	43
毒蛇	dú shé	poisonous snake	43
鳄鱼	è yú	crocodile	43
想念	xiǎng niàn	to miss	43
外婆	wài pó	maternal grandmother	44
住在	zhù zài	to live at (in)	44
西湖	xī hú	West Lake	44

Hanzi	Pinyin	English	Page
桥	qiáo	bridge	44
柳树	liǔ shù	willow trees	44
喜欢	xǐ huan	to like	44
湖上	hú shang	on the lake	44
划船	huá chuán	to row a boat	44
日本	rì běn	Japan	45
海边	hǎi biān	seaside	45
钓鱼	diào yú	fishing	45
海鲜	hǎi xiān	seafood	45
尤其	yóu qí	especially	45
沙西米	shā xī mǐ	raw fish slices; sashimi	45
非洲	fēi zhōu	Africa	46
水果	shuǐ guǒ	fruit	46
大丰收	dà fēng shōu	big harvest	46

Hanzi	Pinyin	English	Page
…的时候	…de shí hou	at the time of…	46
村民们	cūn mín men	villagers	46
好热闹	hǎo rè nao	very crowded and noisy	46
这里	zhè lǐ	here	47
太平洋	tài píng yáng	Pacific Ocean	48
拣贝壳	jiǎn bèi ké	to pick up seashells	48
看日落	kàn rì luò	to observe the sunset	48
搬	bān	to move	49
Lesson 6			
四海一家	sì hǎi yì jiā	literally means "four seas gather as one family"; one world	52
决定	jué dìng	to decide	52
念书	niàn shū	to study	53
后来	hòu lái	later	53

Hanzi	Pinyin	English	Page
认识	rèn shí	to be acquainted with; to know someone	53
留	liú	to stay	53
公司	gōng sī	company	54
工程师	gōng chéng shī	engineer	54
派	pài	to assign	54
护士	hù shì	nurse	55
医生	yī shēng	doctor	55
出生	chū shēng	was born	55
环境	huán jìng	environment	56
世界各地	shì jiè gè dì	everywhere in the world	56
建立	jiàn lì	to establish	56
长大以后	zhǎng dà yǐ hòu	after...having grown up	57
不管	bù guǎn	no matter; regardless	57

Hanzi	Pinyin	English	Page
永远	yǒng yuǎn	always; forever	57
宝贵	bǎo guì	precious	57
知识	zhī shi	knowledge	57
决心	jué xīn	determination	57

我会…… I Can…

I can...

1. use a variety of adjectives to describe a person —————— ☐

2. identify some places beyond my community —————— ☐

3. tell someone the story of Hua Mulan —————— ☐

4. talk about one or two big ideals I learned from Hua Mulan's story ☐

5. explain some important Chinese concepts such as 孝顺 or 四海一家 ☐

6. talk about my hometown and an experience I had when I was little ☐

7. show that I know and appreciate some things about my own cultural heritage and also the heritage of others —————— ☐

8. identify a few occupations and pastimes in different environments, such as hunting, fishing, farming, etc. —————— ☐

9. sing a Chinese song about my home —————— ☐

10. use the *hanzi* in this book, in combination with Hanyu Pinyin, to write labels, signs, or notes. I can do this either by handwriting or using the keyboard. —————— ☐